A Workbook for Pre-Marriage and Those Re-Entering Marriage

Who Am I

About to Marry

By Pattie Atkinson Scotto

Who Am I About to Marry?

Workbook for Pre-Marriage

&

Those Re-entering Marriage

~~~~~~~~~~~~~~~~~~~~~~~~

©2017 Pattie Atkinson Scotto

ISBN 978-1-387-20070-2

Cover Design **by Pamela Tremblay EDS, LPC**

Editing, formatting and layout by **Theresa DiStefano RN, BSHA**

~~~~~~~~~~~~~~~~~~~~~~~~~

Acknowledgements

Thanks to my friend **Theresa DiStefano RN, BSHA**, without her format and counsel this workbook would not be ready for print.

Thanks to **Pamela Scotto Tremblay, BA, MED, EDS, ND, LPC** for her assistance and creativeness of the concept for the cover and the execution of the ISBN Number.

Thanks also to **Patricia Ann Nay, BA, MED, EDS**, for her unwavering enthusiasm and support concerning the publishing of this book.

Dedication

To all those entering marriage and a special dedication to all those re-entering marriage.

~~~~~~~~~~~~~~~~~~~~~~

Table of Contents

Introduction 9

Using the Workbook 10

Basic Issues in Marriage 11

Who Am I About to Marry? 15

    Families -Time Spent with Families.. 18
    Finances – Responsibility, Accountability 21
    Spirituality - Relationship with God.. 24
    Sexuality - Faithfulness and Monogamy 27
    Parenting - Shared Values 28
    Careers - Equal Treatment and Respect 29

Differences Between You.. 32

Character Traits 37

Self- Awareness Inventory 40

Marriage Issues 43

Communication Openness, Honesty   First issue that troubles a marriage.................. 43

Parallel Lives - Second issue that troubles a marriage 49

    Same Plane... 50
    When were we on the same plane? 50
    Becoming a Wife or Husband 53
    Good Wolf - Bad Wolf... 55
    Parallel Plane 57
    Procrastination.. 59

Priorities – What's Important? - Third issue that trouble a marriage......................... 60

Criticism 64

How do you repair a marriage? 65

Cold Feet 66

History of Marriage.. 70

Love Is... True Happiness... 72

Do not allow anyone or anything to come between you and your love. It is rare to find!........................... 72

Unconditional Love.. 72

Letter Poems 75

    Daylight Ending- Stowe, Vermont 75
    Sunlight Shadows 76

Giacomo Puccini - La Rondine...77

Fountain of Life 78

Spot Lighting 79

Stormy Sky 80

Artwork 81

Evening Time 82

Lefkada, Greece- Poem 1 83

Lefkada, Greece – Poem #2 85

Spartacus...86

Sunset Spotlight..87

Die Walkure (1856)-The Ring of Nibelungs-The Valkyrie 88

Jerusalem 89

Golden Hue 90

Bless Us Tonight..91

Grey Sky 92

Peter and the Fish..93

Corfu, Greek Cafe 94

Bethlehem 96

One Foundation 98

Letters 99

Who Am I About to Marry: by Charlotte 99

I Was Happily Married for 23 Years and Want That Again: By Lea................... 101

HI, My Name is Robert, ... 103

About the Author 104

~~~~~~~~~~~~~~~~~~~~~~~

Introduction

Love and Marriage go together. Love has no boundaries and because of this fact it causes many individuals to ask the question what is this thing called "love"? Love is the recognition of goodness which is a desire of the heart. Love because it has no boundaries, causes many individuals to search for limits to feel grounded. Many individuals have heard he or she is my "soul mate" and that is because not only does the physical side of love exist but so does the spiritual side when recognized. It is the spiritual side which is infinite.

When two individuals are in love they are in a different reality. Many have heard the saying, "**_They have on rose-colored glasses!_**" **It is because of this phenomenon that I have written this workbook. It is imperative you thoroughly look at who has captured your heart.** The following questions within this workbook will be fun to answer and explore together and will help you both understand each other better when your rose-colored glasses come off.

Marriage is a major decision. **_Why_ and _to whom_ you are about to marry are major decisions. The following workbook questions will assist you both concerning your decisions before entering or _re-entering_ marriage.**

The workbook will encourage you to examine the _what and why_ of your opinions and identifies your beliefs associated with your opinions. **Completing this workbook will be a very beneficial exercise <u>before</u> you marry.** The format of the workbook is simple. There are questions for **<u>both of you</u>** to answer. There are no wrong answers because truth wins every time. By answering the questions in this workbook, you will develop a better understanding of each other concerning your marriage.

Marriage is not something that comes natural. It is not the product of inborn behavioral patterns. Marriage is an ancient institution and is a cluster of Customs, Traditions, Religious and Social Definitions along with Legal Restrictions. **By answering the questions in this workbook, you will develop a better understanding of each other concerning your marriage.**

~~~~~~~~~~~~~~~~~~~~~~~~

Using the Workbook

The workbook offers a safe place for self-discovery for you AND of who you are about to marry. The format of the workbook is simple. You will be asked to write answers in the workbook to specific self-discovery questions regarding who you are and who you are about to marry. **There are questions for both of you to answer.** Once you have answered the questions you will be able to discover by your answers what married life might be like with each other. Both of you will have a better idea of your compatibility for living together. The self-discovery questions will give you better insight of who you are and who you are about to marry. *Knowing a little bit more about your fiancée than what you know now will assist you long after you are married.*

While writing your answers in the workbook you will need more space to write your answers. Have a separate journal handy to write your entire answer or simply complete what you started in the workbook. Either way, always date the page in your journal and the page number from the workbook referencing the question answered. Journaling along with your answers in the workbook will help you to clarify a personal belief about yourself and others. It forces you to examine your opinions and identifies your beliefs associated with your opinions.

Ideally each of you would have your own separate workbook and journal to respond to the questions. This way keeps the responses real and honest for each of you, as well, you can share *what* you are willing to share *when* you are ready to share. It also minimizes the temptation for one of you writing the responses for the other. However, one workbook can be used for both of your answers, but each should have their own journal.

⚠ **Once all the questions in the workbook have been completed by both of you, review together each question with both of your answers. Any answers to the questions that are not in harmony with each other should be noted and marked in your workbook and journal with a plus sign. At the end of each section, review each question marked with a plus sign. Each plus sign must be discussed until you both reach a solution for why the plus sign was marked in your workbook and/or journal.**

~~~~~~~~~~~~~~~~~~~~~~

Basic Issues in Marriage

An awareness gained by completing this workbook will assist you long after married life begins.

When you are in love nothing seems to matter concerning the issues that are part of marriage. However, you *will* be facing many issues once you are married and we will cover the main issues in this workbook. Entering marriage without facing these important basic issues will be devastating to learn after the fact that you and your fiancée do not agree on the following:

> ➤ Families – *time spent with families*
>
> ➤ Finances - *responsibilities, accountability*
>
> ➤ Spirituality - *relationship with God*
>
> ➤ Sexuality - *faithfulness and monogyny*
>
> ➤ Parenting - *shared values*
>
> ➤ Careers - *equal treatment and respect*

Later, in the workbook we will discuss:

> ➤ Communication - *openness, honesty*
>
> ➤ Parallel Lives – *shared & separate interests*
>
> ➤ Priorities - *what is important*

Keep in mind being attentive and listening to each other's answers is crucial because once you are married your answers could cause conflict. Constant conflicts could and have for others destroyed their marriage. The other day a woman said to me, *"We really get along with each other in our marriage except when we argue"*.

Before we discuss the issues that will become evident in your marriage, let us start with the first important statement of this book:

One should be healed emotionally and psychologically of other past relationships before getting married.

In the workbook *"Conquering Divorce with God"* (available on Amazon) accepting the inevitable and letting go of past relationships is the last step in the healing process. Breakups of serious relationships and the dissolution of marriages have in common emotional consequences such as emotional pain, lack of self-confidence, lack of faith, and anger issues. **Consequences often happen in breakups by looking the other way from negative behaviors.**

You know what did not work out with your other relationships and if you do not know what happened in those relationships, you will know after you complete the relationship section in this workbook. This section will show you a pattern of why you chose to be in those relationships.

Be aware of other traits such as jealousy, greed, narcissism, lust, and control. If this is the first time you have seen these behaviors, they are called "**red flags**". You will find those red flags **almost impossible** to live with and they tend to need professional counseling for correction. If you have seen those behaviors in other relationships, you know they are not constructive and you know the outcome.

Red flags need to be addressed before marriage.

~~~~~~~~~~~~~~~~~~~~~~~

Interdependent

Once you were dependent as a child, then you became independent, but now you are looking for a partner where you both will be interdependent. Interdependent means to depend mutually on each other. Interdependent allows you to rely on each other with neither of you being needy. By being interdependent and trusting with each other, you will be able to rely with total confidence on each other. By having total confidence with each other you will develop implicit faith and total belief in each other. By being able to confide, trust, have confidence, faith, and total belief with each other, you both will develop a moral responsibility to each other.

Vignette

There was a man who described interdependency as two trees growing side by side. The trees stay two trees but in time the roots become intertwined where they became a single source for life.

There is no rush to make a lifelong commitment to who you think the person is by not recognizing who they are in the illusion, fantasy, infatuation and thinking you are in love. If this happens the illusion, fantasy, or infatuation will not be enough to save the marriage. In time, because the relationship was not built on friendship and companionship, the relationship will dissolve.

Vignette

There was a woman who was overjoyed to be married to a man who not only had children, but grandchildren too, as she always wanted children. They had a large wedding of 700 guests. When they were at the alter and it was time to exchange rings he would not take off his dead wife's ring. The marriage lasted three years.

Couples sometimes *appear* to love each other but cannot live together without causing damage to each other. Companionship and the ability to communicate will counteract not being able to live together. Companionship and communication develop a deep connection that binds a couple in an intimate union with imperishable strength for a lifetime of marriage.

~~~~~~~~~~~~~~~~~~~~~~

Who Am I About to Marry?

During the engagement, you have committed and declared your love for each other, but how well do you know each other? Taking time to know who you are about to marry is imperative because there is so much excitement when you finally agree to marry. After the engagement and the starting of the wedding plans, there is little time to stop and contemplate who the individual is that you are about to marry.

The planning of a wedding is a whirlwind and considering who you are about to marry is not included in the planning. Having a basic agreement with each other of your wedding plans is desirable as it will not always be that way once you are married. Married life changes a couple and incorporates how each one *"really feels"* about every decision. Decisions in marriage at times become a little more complex. A basic agreement is when you both agree on a decision. The more unified you are the more compatible you become as a couple. The word unity literally means *"joined, combined, agreement in harmony"*. When a marriage is built on a foundation of love and mutual agreements, the marriage is in a happier state. Unity is not saying "yes" when you mean "no". An agreement means that both of you will say "yes" when you mean yes thus finding common ground.

Vignette

Louise always thought she had to agree with her fiancée. If he said, he would like Italian food for dinner and she preferred Chinese food she would give into Italian food. If one of the partners would have offered another suggestion such as Mexican food or Indian food, a compromise on a third alternative could have led to an agreement.

When you are falling in love you do not see anything that would cause disagreement between the two of you once you are married, however, there are many areas that could cause disagreement. We will address those issues that will affect your marriage.

Love is enough when you take the time to discover who you are about to marry. It is important that both of you have the emotional capacity to share your lives with each other.

It is time to begin the exercises in the workbook. Remember you will need a journal for more space to write your answers. Have your journal handy to complete your answers in the workbook always dating the page in your journal and the page of your question that you are answering in the workbook. The questions will be addressed to you and your fiancée.

There are several reasons people decide to marry: *for love, economics, and security, desire of a home and children, parents, escape from loneliness, money, companionship and many more.*

What are the reasons that you are getting married?

Fiancée - Explain: _____

_____

_____

_____

_____

Fiancée- Explain: _____

_____

_____

_____

What would you say that you both have in common?

Fiancée - Explain: _____

_____

_____

_____

_____

Fiancée- Explain: _____

_____

_____

_____

What would you like to share with your fiancée that maybe they don't know?

Fiancée - Explain: _____

_____

_____

Fiancée- Explain: _____

_____

_____

What was the deciding factor to marry your fiancée?

Fiancée – Explain: _____

_____

_____

Fiancée - Explain _____

_____

_____

_____

The next section of the workbook addresses common issues couples face and should be discussed before entering a marriage. Clearly journaling each other's intentions will help you both understand each other and be well prepared for those difficult times when issues occur.

~~~~~~~~~~~~~~~~~~~~~~~~

Families -Time Spent with Families

Vignette

There was a man who divorced his wife. They had 3 girls ages 5, 7, and 10 when they separated. He loved his children. The mother and girls moved from Georgia to South Carolina without notice to her husband. They had joint custody. He remarried before everything was settled. The girls and their mother moved again from South Carolina to Tennessee where every Friday night the father drove to Tennessee from Georgia to see his children. Often the schedule was disrupted by the children's mother.

If there are children from a former marriage do you have a calendar for major holidays and visits that will be accepted by the other parent? Explain: _____

_____

_____

How does each of you perceive sharing your time with visits to your families?

Fiancée - Explain: _____

_____

_____

Fiancée - Explain: _____

_____

_____

Did either of you share with each other a calendar of dates concerning your families and the major holidays visits? Explain: _____

_____

_____

_____

If there are children from a former marriage do you have a calendar for major holidays and visits that will be accepted by the other parent? Explain: _____

_____

_____

How often did you decide to visit each parent?

Fiancée - Explain: _____

_____

_____

Fiancée - Explain: _____

_____

_____

Do both of you enjoy visiting each other's parents?

Fiancée - Explain: _____

_____

_____

Fiancée - Explain: _____

_____

_____

If the answer is not yes for both of you, what will you do to try to find a way to incorporate each other's parents with positive visits?

Fiancée - Explain: _____

_____

_____

Fiancée - Explain: _____

_____

_____

If there is a family member who does not get along with one or either of you, what can you do to help the situation? Explain: _____

_____

_____

_____

_____

_____

_____

_____

_____

_____

_____

_____

_____

_____

_____

_____

~~~~~~~~~~~~~~~~~~~~~~

Finances – Responsibility, Accountability

If one of you is coming into the marriage with more assets, how will you both determine what should be done with those assets? Will you share them with each other? Will you share evenly? Will you decide each has their own nest egg? Explain: _____

_____

_____

_____

_____

If one of you is coming into the marriage with more debt, how will you both determine what should be done with that debt? Will you share the debt? Will you share evenly? Will you decide each has their own debt to be responsible for? Explain: _____

_____

_____

_____

_____

If one of you is making more money than the other, will their money be used by the other? Will they have open access to it? Explain: _____

_____

_____

_____

_____

If one of you is making more money than the other, will that money be used to pay off any possible debt brought into the marriage by the other? Explain: _____

_____

_____

_____

_____

Will you have two separate bank accounts in your marriage? Explain: _____

_____

_____

_____

_____

Will you have a joint savings account? Explain: _____

_____

_____

_____

_____

Will you have separate and joint accounts? Explain: _____

_____

_____

_____

Will there be a joint account to be used for the mortgage, utilities, food, and monthly expenses?

Explain: _____

_____

_____

_____

If you have joint accounts will one or the other or both be responsible for reconciling it? How will it be

reconciled? Explain: _____

_____

_____

_____

_____

If a bill is not paid and a late charge is incurred who will pay for it or will it come from a joint account that

each of you contribute to? Explain: _____

_____

_____

_____

_____

If you both are contributing to a joint account will the amounts be the same even if one makes more money

than the other? Explain: _____

_____

_____

_____

Will you or each of you be considering buying life insurance in case something happens to your partner?
How much insurance should you have? Who will be responsible for purchasing it? Who will be responsible
for making payment toward it? Who will be beneficiary? Explain: _____

_____

_____

_____

_____

~~~~~~~~~~~~~~~~~~~~~~~~~

Spirituality - Relationship with God

The Sacramental side of a marriage is very important for unity. It is the foundation of truth and honesty governed by God. If one believed and knew God, the desire for material wealth would not overpower one's values and become the focal point of a marriage. Going to a place of worship is a happy experience. Most of us were taught right from wrong in those surroundings. In marriage by sharing in a Sacramental union you become "one Flesh" _(Mark10:7-8)_. Even our legal system recognizes that the husband-wife relationship is not two entirely distant persons. They cannot testify against each other.

About twenty years ago, I wrote a book but did not publish it, but I am still thinking of doing so! I wrote it because as a Corporate Recruiter in Corporate America there were applicants who honestly did not know what they wanted to do, nor did they know right from wrong. I went home and started and finished a book called, _"What If There Is a God?"_ I made copies for a while and handed them out! If the simple question of not knowing right from wrong cannot be answered, then putting God in the equation of marital values seems almost impossible. God becomes a real necessity at this point for the understanding of right from wrong.

Do either of you have a religious foundation?

Fiancée - Explain: _____

_____

Fiancée - Explain: _____

_____

Do either of you intend to attend a place of worship? Explain: _____

_____

If either of you are Catholic and are re-entering marriage, do you or your fiancée have an annulment?

Explain: _____

_____

_____

Let us consider what is love, where does it come from? In marriage love is affectionate, engaging with a passionate and devoted attachment. Love cannot be seen, touched or manufactured. Only through us do we know love exists. Love is not outside of you, **love is inside of you.** When there is a disconnect there is no love. Love is a connection. God is love, and we are created in His image.

Who is God? Saint Paul tells us who God is through a letter St. Paul wrote to the Corinthians.   God is love. Since God is love the following describes who God is, *"Love is patient, it is not jealous, it is not pompous, it is not inflated, it is not rude, it does not seek its own interests, it is not quick-tempered, it does not brood over injury, it does not rejoice over wrongdoing but rejoices with the truth, it bears all things, believes all things, hopes all things, endure all things. Love never fails." (1 Corinthians 13:4-8).*

This description of love always had me coming up short.   If I was pleasant one day and the next day I was rude or one day I was quick tempered and the next day not, it seemed I never had all the traits at one time. I must tell you for years I thought I had to have all those traits daily and my partner too! However, thank goodness, I learned that St. Paul was describing what God was and I felt so much better.

"As you move closer to God you can invest more love in yourself and you will find it easier to love others."

~~~St. John of The Cross

It is difficult to love others if we do not love ourselves. Reaching out to love our neighbor is important even if it is not returned because so many have never known love. By showing love, the love of God in you gives you the strength to lift the hearts of those without hope. Sometimes it takes a lot of love for our neighbors to feel worthy.

Saying I am sorry to God is a win-win behavior because God always forgives us if we truly repent. God's love is unconditional. Remember to say, "I am sorry" to your partner whenever an apology is needed.

In college, I took an elective course on marriage, when the discussion was on similar backgrounds for a successful marriage I knew opposites attract, so how could we choose someone similar? I learned eventually that similar interests are important in marriage. If a man or woman likes to read and the other partner does not have an interest in reading there will be tension over the partner finding time to read. Or how about fishing where the other partner does not like fishing at all, as it may be too quiet and time-consuming? Of course, if the partner who doesn't like fishing likes to read it may be a perfect match!

Think about what your interests are and what your fiancée interests are:

Fiancée -Interests

Explain: _____

_____

_____

Fiancée – Interests

Explain: _____

_____

_____

~~~~~~~~~~~~~~~~~~~~~~~~

Sexuality - Faithfulness and Monogamy

Waiting is optimum for sex before marriage. Sex, intimacy, and love are all different. When one becomes sexually intimate after knowing someone only a short time you short circuit everything else. You have had no time to build a foundation based on respect, trust, communication, understanding, and friendship. When the relationship calms down there will be nothing between the two of you to sustain the relationship. You must become aware that using sex to fill a void, pretending it is love, is reckless and lust at best.

Sex is often disguised as intimacy. Becoming best friends and soul mates cannot happen because there has been no time to grow together. Intimacy begins with you which will make you more capable of sharing with another person. Intimacy brings out the respect for yourself, self-worth, value, and dignity. Do not do anything unwillingly that will cause you to lose either your integrity or self-respect.

You cannot speed up or hurry the meeting of the right person for marriage. If you do not wait for the right person, the wounds could be long lasting from dating the wrong individuals. It is not only futile; it could be dangerous and self-destructive. Moral responsibility will put the brakes on a relationship of lust.

~~~~~~~~~~~~~~~~~~~~~~~~

Parenting - Shared Values

Children are a blessing! Knowing the parenting method your fiancée was brought up with, will help you understand their parenting skill. There are so many methods and they can really clash between the two of you.

Are you strict or lenient?

Fiancée - Explain: _____

_____

_____

_____

_____

_____

Fiancée - Explain: _____

_____

_____

_____

_____

_____

Some parents have a spreadsheet schedule for their child. Others allow the child to dictate their schedule. There could be issues down to breast feeding or formula feedings for your babies. You may not think this an important issue, but let me assure you if you both do not agree on your parenting style, your children as they grow up will use your differences to their advantage.

~~~~~~~~~~~~~~~~~~~~~~~

Careers - Equal Treatment and Respect

There are many issues to discuss. Will either of you want to finish a degree? If so will it be a High School, Trade School or College degree? An Associate, Bachelors, Masters, Doctorate, MD degree or something else?

Fiancée - Explain: _____

_____

Fiancée- Explain: _____

_____

How many years to finish your degree will it take?

Fiancée - Explain: _____

_____

Fiancée- Explain: _____

_____

How will it be financed?

Fiancée - Explain: _____

_____

Fiancée - Explain: _____

_____

If you are a professional, how many hours will you be working a week?

Fiancée - Explain: _____

_____

Fiancée- Explain: _____

_____

If you are a tradesman, or working in a company or hospital or hotel, how many hours a week will you be working?

Fiancée - Explain: _____

_____

Fiancée - Explain: _____

_____

When promotions are offered in another State will you relocate?

Fiancée - Explain: _____

_____

Fiancée - Explain: _____

_____

Vignette

There was a young executive recently divorced who was promoted and needed to relocate from Atlanta to Texas. He did not want to leave our Divorce and Separated support group. I explained to him that he had to go because if he turned this position down there might not be another opportunity. My career was an Executive Recruiter for Fortune 500 Companies. The larger the company the less they work with what a person wants for their career. This was a large oil company. I made a list of things he could do when he was lonely to take with him. He relocated to Houston, Texas. He made phone calls to us until he felt settled. He eventually married after three years and they have a son. It has been 16 years and his son is now 12 years old. He sends a family Christmas card every year and they are very happy.

Where will you find time for your marriage after working daily and a commute home?

Fiancée - Explain: _____

_____

Fiancée - Explain: _____

_____

Who will prepare the meals?

Fiancée - Explain: _____

_____

Fiancée - Explain: _____

_____

How will the household chores be divided up?

Fiancée - Explain: _____

_____

_____

Fiancée - Explain: _____

_____

_____

What will come first, marriage or career?

Fiancée - Explain: _____

_____

_____

Fiancée - Explain: _____

_____

_____

~~~~~~~~~~~~~~~~~~~~~~~~

Differences Between You

It is important when you become aware of differences between you and your partner that you communicate with your partner as soon as these differences arise. Maybe what you want your partner to *be* may not be what your partner is *today*, and may never *become*. Before you marry, you must accept the person the way they are.

There cannot be any delusions that any one individual can change another individual.

Trying to mold or "train" our partners into what we want is never a long-lasting change.

A person can only truly change from a spiritual awakening within themselves.

There are misconceptions about what marriage is? Many people in love think that the marriage union performed at the wedding ceremony will prepare one after the ceremony for the experience of marriage. Unfortunately, it will not prepare you. There are others who think marriage will be like an extension of the courtship, filled with flowers, attention, and poems, unfortunately, it is not. It is possible that on your anniversary, holiday, or birthday your spouse may or may not remember flowers, dinner, and/or a card.

Marriage unites two individuals into one unit, blending two but not taking away each one's individuality. It often occurs while dating that...

...one of the partners gives up their individuality to the other, and once married there is a struggle to take back their individuality.

Married life begins with many decisions made by both of you. Most of your life up until now have not required more than you in the decisions in your daily life. This is not an easy transition. You will be surprised to discover that there might be differences between the two of you where you will live, what furniture styles you both agree on, what car to purchase and what colors of paint and carpeting you both will choose for your home. This is the beginning of the give and take of marriage.

The questions in this self-discovery workbook have been written to help you realize before the ceremony of marriage, issues that you might want to uncover with your fiancée. The questions will give you a better insight to assist you in marriage.

If you have lived with your fiancée before marriage do not confuse this experience like being married. Once your vows are declared the metamorphous begins. There will be a transformation in form and nature between the two of you.

Before the wedding date, hopefully you will have had your first big argument and not just a disagreement to understand how the other person reacts in an argument. In this first argument, you will discover if you or your fiancée are cold and withdrawn keeping the anger in, or if you and your fiancée are explosive showing outwardly the anger. You will discover if you or your fiancée are trying to control each other or if either of you were pathological in the premise of the argument. Did you or your fiancée have to be right just to be right, or were either of you disinterested? Did either of you push each other because if either of you did push, hitting might come next?

Arguing is very telling of who you and your fiancée are under the layers. Reactions and methods will never change unless there is an understanding of who influenced the behavior or what was witnessed by either of you in your past.

The following exercises in the workbook will bring to the forefront what happened to you and your fiancée's decisions from each personal relationship in your past and the outcome of each decision. It will also give you a new understanding of how and why each of you will react and make decisions in the future. Look for a pattern such as did you or your fiancée walk away from a relationship or did you choose individuals that left either of you? If it were the latter, did anyone in his or her family walk away from responsibility? Or if it was the former, did either of you experience being hurt and never wanting to be that close to anyone so not to be hurt again?

The following questions are for both of you to answer.

When was the first time you fell in love? What happened to that relationship? Why didn't that relationship

work out? Explain: _____

_____

_____

_____

Recall all dating relationships and what happened and why those relationships didn't work out? Explain:

_____

_____

_____

Have you ever had an argument with a friend? What did you argue about? Explain: _____

_____

_____

_____

Recall all of you and your fiancée's friend's arguments, and write how they worked out and use your journal

if necessary for more space. Explain: _____

_____

_____

_____

Have you or your fiancée argued together with parents, mother, or father? If so how did it end? Explain:

_____

_____

_____

Recall all arguments that you or your fiancée had separately with your parents and write how those

arguments worked out. Explain: _____

_____

_____

_____

What traits of other members of your families did you see in your arguments? Explain: _____

_____

_____

_____

There are loving moms, critical moms, alcoholic moms, death of their moms and abusive moms. What

traits of each of your mothers did you see in your arguments? Explain: _____

_____

_____

I see traits of my mother in me. Good Traits: _____

_____

_____

Bad Traits: _____

_____

There are loving dads, controlling dads, alcoholic dads, abusive dads, and absent dads. What traits of each

of your fathers did you see in your arguments? Explain: _____

_____

_____

_____

_____

I see traits of my Father in me? Good Traits: _____

_____

_____

Bad Traits: _____

_____

_____

Was there anyone close to you in your past growing up whose traits are evident in your decision making or

behavior? Explain: _____

_____

_____

_____

_____

_____

_____

_____

_____

_____

_____

~~~~~~~~~~~~~~~~~~~~~~~~

Character Traits

In this section, you will do an exercise to help you identify the various character traits each of you possess and ultimately will share in your marriage. One should become aware of the character traits within themselves and within the individual they are going to marry.

Step 1: --Each of you should check the words that apply to yourself. *There are blank spaces at bottom of the list for you to add more words that best describes each of you.*

	His	Her		His	Her
Likes Control	_____	_____	Enjoys Routine	_____	_____
Bold	_____	_____	Loyal	_____	_____
Goal Driven	_____	_____	Even Keeled	_____	_____
Strong Willed	_____	_____	Dislikes Change	_____	_____
Self-reliant	_____	_____	Dry Humor	_____	_____
Takes Charge	_____	_____	Nurturing	_____	_____
Determined	_____	_____	Tolerant	_____	_____
Indecisive	_____	_____	Peace Maker	_____	_____
Inspirational	_____	_____	Analytical	_____	_____
Competitive	_____	_____	Precise	_____	_____
Adventurous	_____	_____	Scheduled	_____	_____
Energetic	_____	_____	Deliberate	_____	_____
Fun-loving	_____	_____	Reserved	_____	_____
Optimistic	_____	_____	Perfectionist	_____	_____
Risk Taker	_____	_____	Accurate	_____	_____
Likes Change	_____	_____	Orderly	_____	_____
Non-demanding	_____	_____	Spontaneous	_____	_____
_____	_____	_____	_____	_____	_____
_____	_____	_____	_____	_____	_____
_____	_____	_____	_____	_____	_____
_____	_____	_____	_____	_____	_____

Step 2: Once each of you have completed going through the list, if your fiancée does not mark a word that you think *or know* describes them put a plus sign (+) by the word for later discussion. *Also, put a plus sign next to the words each of you has identified for each other that were not on the list.*

Step 3: Now make a list of all the individual words identified by **her.** Do the same for **his** words in the columns below. *Also include those words identified with the plus sign and keep them noted with the plus sign.*

Her list   **His list**

_____   _____

_____   _____

_____   _____

_____   _____

_____   _____

_____   _____

_____   _____

_____   _____

There are so many other words that are not on the list, feel free to list them as you discover them.

Step 4: Review the lists. Are there **opposite** words describing who you are and who your fiancée is? *For example, one likes control and the other is self-willed; or if one is indecisive and the other is precise?*

Step 5: Cross reference all the words from **Her** list to **His**. Review **Her** list one word at a time to **His** list one word at a time; closely review each word line after line. If there are words found to be incompatible write them in the space marked **Incompatible Words**.

Continued

Continued step 5

Incompatible Words

_____   _____   _____

_____   _____   _____

_____   _____   _____

Step 6: Once you have identified all the incompatible words go back to your journals and explain in depth how each trait would detract or enhance a marriage and what each trait would be like to live with every day in marriage. How will these traits play out in everyday life?

Step 7: Most importantly you must devote time to discuss how these specific incompatibilities will work out in your home. Discuss the incompatible words one by one until you both find a solution to their incompatibility.

What have you discovered in comparing your words?

Explain_____

_____

_____

_____

_____

_____

_____

_____

_____

~~~~~~~~~~~~~~~~~~~~~~~

Self- Awareness Inventory

The questions below are for both of you to answer

Perception is often mistaken as a reality for an individual. What does that sentence mean to you?

Fiancée - Explain: _____

_____

_____

Fiancée- Explain: _____

_____

_____

One example of perception is during the courtship people exhibit a behavior, such as being more fun, entertaining, and charming. However, after the marriage he or she may have a more serious nature and may not be as much fun, charming or entertaining. Choosing a partner for life should never occur under the influence of alcohol as one's perception is distorted. Do you know who you are marring?

Give three examples describing what you know of your fiancée.

1. _____

2. _____

3. _____

Give three examples of what makes you unhappy?

1. _____

2. _____

3. _____

What are the three things that would make you happy?

1. _____

2. _____

3. _____

Do you have any boundaries? Name three of your boundaries and explain each one. (Another word for boundaries is limits.)

1. _____

2. _____

3. _____

Since you met your intended have your boundaries changed? Explain: _____

_____

_____

Why do you think anyone has boundaries? Explain: _____

_____

_____

What are your core values? Name your top three core values and explain each one. *(Another word for core values is worth.)*

1. _____

2. _____

3. _____

Have any of your core values changed since you met your intended? Explain: _____

_____

What are your principles? *(Another word for principals is morals.)* Name your top three principles and explain each.

1. _____

2. _____

3. _____

Have any of your principles changed since you met your intended? Explain: _____

_____

_____

_____

To what extent has anyone violated your boundaries, core values or principles? If so what did you do about this situation? Explain: _____

_____

_____

_____

_____

_____

_____

_____

_____

_____

_____

_____

_____

_____

~~~~~~~~~~~~~~~~~~~~~~~

Marriage Issues

The three main issues that trouble a marriage are:

Number One: **Communication - *Openness, Honesty***

Number Two: **Parallel Planes – *Shared & Separate Interests***

Number Three: **Priorities – *What is Important***

Each issue will be addressed separately starting with **communication** which is the most difficult yet the simplest it would seem of the three main issues that trouble a marriage.

Communication Openness, Honesty - First issue that troubles a marriage.

It is a big help if you use subjects, predicates, and objects when trying to communicate effectively. Obtaining the other person's attention is **<u>critical</u>** because if they are partly engaged half way through what you are saying, the outcome will not be what either of you wanted!

Men like <u>to solve problems.</u> Simply expecting them to *listen* to problems tends to lose their attention. I learned years ago, that I had to use a subject! For example, instead of saying, *"You know I was upset today".* He wonders <u>*why*</u> at first and it takes a few minutes for him to figure out what I am saying to engage with me. However, if I had identified from the start what was upsetting me such as, *"<u>Jennifer</u> upset me today",* my partner would know from the beginning why I was upset.

When you want to communicate, it is better to be side by side than facing each other. When you come up to your partner face to face they immediately go on the defense. When you think, you were not understood ask them to repeat what you said so there will not be any question if your partner heard you.

Remember *<u>hearing</u>* what is said is paramount to communication!

The questions below are for both of you to answer.

Before you communicate with your fiancée or someone at work, why should you get their attention before

the communication starts? Explain: _____

_____

_____

_____

Why when communicating is the *tone of voice the* two people use very important? Explain: _____

_____

_____

_____

The single most important of the three major reasons that trouble a marriage is <u>communication</u>.

Why is communication important in a marriage? Explain: _____

_____

The expectations of marriage that are met will lead to improving communication. Why would meeting

expectations be important? Explain: _____

_____

No one is a mind reader and disappointments can be averted if both partners "hear" what their partner is

saying when they are communicating. Why would this be important? Explain: _____

Good communication is the root of happiness in a marriage.

Who Am I About to Marry?

What are your expectations of a husband or wife? Explain: _____

_____

_____

What are your expectations of marriage? Explain: _____

_____

_____

How similar are you and your fiancée's expectations of marriage? Explain: _____

_____

_____

What will be the result of your union if your expectations are different? Explain: _____

_____

_____

Do you understand the differences between passive and aggressive behavior? Explain: _____

_____

_____

What is passive behavior? Explain: _____

_____

_____

With passive behavior, did you know there is a fear of disapproval or rejection? Explain: _____

_____

_____

Do you or your fiancée have indirect hostility that is evident for something your fiancée or someone else did that upset either of you? Explain: _____

_____

_____

Every time you or your fiancée promise and do not follow through on what you have agreed to, you lose

credibility. Have either of you promised to do something and then did not do it? Explain: _____

_____

_____

What is aggressive behavior? Explain: _____

_____

_____

Why would aggressive behavior require anger management for a happy union? Explain: _____

_____

_____

Do you know what makes your fiancée angry? Explain: _____

_____

_____

What is your fiancée's favorite color, food, and music?   Color_____ Food _____

Music Genre _____

Why is it that in poor communication one could emotionally withdraw, detach, become critical, and have an

unwillingness to co-operate? Explain: _____

_____

Why does every fiancée need to feel important, loved and valued? Explain: _____

_____

_____

Why would your fiancée need attention, affection, be affirmed and appreciated? Explain: _____

_____

_____

Why would poor communication which sometimes have cruel words, leave unnecessary emotional and

mental wounds? Explain: _____

_____

_____

The following lists will assist you in having your fiancée feel loved, valued, important, and appreciated.

Men Need	Women Need
Trust	Caring
Acceptance	Understanding
Appreciation	Respect
Admiration	Devotion
Approval	Validation
Encouragement	Reassurance

Reviewing the words above concerning your fiancée, how often have you both remembered to put into

action the words from the above lists? Explain: _____

_____

_____

_____

Good communication is not easy. In marriage, there are conditions such as worry, stress, fear and anger which can impede the concentration of your partner's attention. Wanting to share something with your partner right away may be the right thing for you to do, but the timing with your partner may be wrong. For example, if he is focused on what he is doing, and you interrupt him, it will take him 30 minutes to get back to finishing what he is doing and time after time of being interrupted will irritate him. If she is busy she will get frustrated as she is probably multi-tasking. Wait until he/she has finished doing what they set out to do, then obtain their attention. Also, keep in mind, there is a possibility you might have to ask them to **repeat** what you have said because what they heard is not what you said because he/she was contemplating other priorities.

Communication is challenged when what is important to one person is not important or interesting to the other person. The next example can only represent a married couple because as a fiancée they trip all over themselves to do anything you ask at the time you ask! Familiarity in marriage has a way of knowing that yesterday the task was not done and that today the task maybe put off until tomorrow.

For example, a window shade needs fixing and it bothers your partner every day when they see it broken. The other partner was asked to fix it, but preferred to think of a business trip, a fishing, or a golf trip, and does not have the broken window shade as a priority to fix. The partner who wants the shade fixed gets irritated each day the shade does not get fixed and the other partner wonders what is wrong with their partner. As simple as the problem is, if it goes unresolved it could affect the partner's emotional feeling toward the other partner. If the other partner discovers the broken shade is why his partner is pulling back, the partner could make his partner feel worse by making his partner feel ridiculous about the broken shade. What is important to the individual must be respected and dealt with when the issue first comes up.

There are so many conditions that contribute to communication and **one thing most of us never consider are the stimuli** of all the sound and sight waves which we are all bombarded with daily. They affect our brain waves in Gamma, Beta, Alpha, Theta and Delta. Therefore, one must obtain your partner's attention before speaking! Communication is made up of words. Choosing the correct words from your thoughts when you speak will facilitate the understanding with your fiancée and later your partner in marriage.

The following thoughts are how a character is developed:
> *"The thought manifests as the word,*
> *The word manifests as the deed,*
> *The deed develops into habit,*
> *And the habit hardens into character.*
> *So, watch the thought and its ways with care,*
> *As we think, so we become."*
> ~~~*Gautama Buddha*

One's **behavior, tone and attitude** of their words can be misunderstood in communication. Address immediately when you see the other person is in a behavior pattern that is upsetting to you and in the future, could cause you or your fiancée harm. **When communication is not understood or even worse when communication is not important to one of the partners in marriage, a new routine evolves, and parallel lives emerge.**

~~~~~~~~~~~~~~~~~~~~~~~

Parallel Lives - Second issue that troubles a marriage

Once you are married and routine has set in, it is common that the time once reserved for the two of you is divided among other interests. It isn't because you do not want to be together all the time, but rather wanting to share some of the time reserved for the two of you in other areas.

If you both agree to find time without each other for seeing old friends and having different interests such as: sewing circles, book of the month club, fishing or building model trains and cars, the two of you will enjoy a healthier relationship. On the other hand, if your partner feels neglected with the amount of time spent outside of the marriage because of your new routine, there is a possibility you will pass each other going and coming which will lead to unhappiness. Address those issues immediately and/or see a counselor. If your partner's interests are not excessive their interests will make for an interesting partner. It is very important to remember if you do not make room for the intimacy of your marriage, you will start to develop a world of your own. This is the beginning of parallel lives.

What are parallel lives you may ask? Parallel lives are when you and your spouse are going in the same direction, but you are on different planes. You may ask how does this happen? It is difficult to explain because before you realize it, it has happened! **Parallel lives are not good for a marriage.** Being aware of parallel lives will help both of you to communicate with each other when a situation is occurring that makes one or both spouses uncomfortable. Before this happens, there are signs to help you both to stay on the same plane. Two questions concerning the same plane or parallel planes are *when were we on the same plane* and *what signs will be seen when either one steps onto a parallel plane?* The first question will be answered below, and the second question will be answered later in this workbook.

Same Plane

When were we on the same plane?

When you first started dating you were on the same plane. You were connected on the same plane by Smartphone, texting, e-mail, making plans for dinner dates, movies, plays, concerts and special events. You were two individuals connecting with as much time that you both had available because you both wanted to be near each other. You could not wait to see one another. You were excited to hear from each other when you answered the phone. You both did small things to surprise each other. You celebrated each other's birthday with a card, a poem, or a gift. You spoke about the future and the commitment to each other. At this stage, you were exclusively dating each other. You both were on the same plane! How many times were you waiting for a phone call or text because you both were on the same plane waiting to make plans for the evening or the week-end to be with each other? **The day started and ended with each other.**

One day the excitement of a proposal of marriage ended the dating phase. The engagement acceptance of *"Will you marry me?"* started the marriage process. The engagement solidified the desires of wanting to be together permanently. **The engagement is the beginning of a whirlwind.** Below is a list of just some of the usual engagement considerations.

If you already have proposed plans and or dates, list each one and when they will be occurring.

Parents will be meeting each other when & where? Date(s) & where: _____

_____

Friends and relatives will be giving engagement parties and bridal parties for you and you will be meeting each other friends. List engagement parties date(s) & where: _____

_____

_____

List bridal showers date(s) & where: _____

_____

_____

You must decide if you will be married in a place of worship, at the beach, or on top of a mountain?

Describe where/venue: _____

Who will be in your bridal party?

Maid/Matron of Honor: _____ Best Man/Woman: _____

Bride Maids: _____

_____

Groomsmen: _____

_____

Will there be others who will have special roles outside the wedding party? _____

_____

_____

You both must decide if it will be a private wedding or a large wedding? _____

How many guests? _____

Where do you draw a line on who is a "guest"? Explain: _____

_____

You must decide who will officiate the marriage vows? _____

_____

A sacramental marriage is a lifelong commitment and has certain requirements. If you are going to be married in a church, you must go and decide with the clergy what steps it will take to be married and while you are there choose a date that is open on the calendar, as the calendar fills up quickly.

Will there be a place of worship you both will be attending? _____

_____

If you are of different faiths will you be attending both services? _____

_____

How often will you be attending worship? Weekly? Bi-weekly? Monthly? Other? _____

After the ceremony, the planning of the reception will be celebrating the most celebrated day of your life!

What date is reserved for your reception? _____

Where will your reception take place? _____

While you both are planning your marriage and reception, time seems to evaporate. It seems like there is never enough of it!   The marriage will make it possible for the two of you to be together, week-in and week-out for the rest of your lives. There will be many decisions like the ones above. Agreeing immediately on each decision is awesome but take note on how you disagree on each decision and how well you reach a compromise. During the engagement compromising is always easier than during marriage.

Take note how you compromise as it will dictate your relationship when you are married!

~~~~~~~~~~~~~~~~~~~~~~~~

Becoming a Wife or Husband

The question, *"what is marriage?"* is often misunderstood. Being part of a "throw-away society," the concept of a lifelong marriage makes it imperative that you ***know*** the person you are going to marry and what the word marriage means. Did you know that during the Sacramental marriage celebration, the marriage vows you both exchange with each other will make the union concrete, permanent, abiding, fixed, imperishable, unchangeable, and enduring? What do those words mean to you? ***Words below are for both of you to answer***.

Concrete _____

_____

Permanent_____

_____

Abiding_____

_____

Fixed_____

_____

Imperishable_____

_____

Unchangeable _____

_____

Enduring_____

_____

Being married has a purpose in our secular and ecclesiastical societies. It is a respected union between two people that have chosen each other. The marriage from the vows through the honeymoon intertwines romance, intimacy, and love in a solid manner of unity between the two of you. There is a security in being married that changes both of you. Belonging to the person of your dreams will cause you **BOTH** to settle down in your new permanent security. *"What do you understand about becoming ......a wife or husband?"*

_____

_____

Somewhere in the security of *"belonging"* in the marriage, one's "dating appearance" of looking one's best is replaced by comfort. Concerning the wife, make-up is the first to go and then the dating clothes are replaced by sweat suits and favorite worn clothes, thus the transformation of the wife has begun! Women change more in appearance than men, although many men may not give up their favorite worn clothes or worn fishing, golf or rain hat. Men are visual creatures. In the beginning, a husband is so much in love with his wife, he does not react to her change in appearance because of his rose-colored glasses but soon coupled with the trials of life he starts to take notice of the transformation of his wife. Combing one's hair should not be an issue for either of you, but it will be in time. No one seems to have time to take this into consideration! Before you greet your wife or husband at the end of the day, comb your hair, put on clean non-wrinkled clothes and wear shoes or flip-flops to the dinner table! Marriage seems to give permission to behave badly 24/7 rather than their charming self, which may be different from what you thought they were like when you were dating.

~~~~~~~~~~~~~~~~~~~~~~~

Good Wolf - Bad Wolf

Like all of us, we have a good wolf and a bad wolf within us.... and when we are dating we never see the bad wolf, but if we do see the bad wolf we make excuses for their behavior which enables the behavior even more. We do not know which wolf or wolves are fed by our partner but we know the wolves or wolf we feed. It is the surprises of who we are and who we married that surfaces in a marriage that can be alarming. Hopefully, each couple brings out the best in each other and not the worst. Even if it is the latter, the love between you both can be shown and communicated to defuse whatever the individual or individuals are going through.

What do you feed your good wolf?

Fiancée - Explain: _____

_____

_____

_____

Fiancée - Explain: _____

_____

_____

_____

What do you feed your bad wolf?

Fiancée - Explain: _____

_____

_____

_____

Fiancée - Explain: _____

_____

_____

_____

Marriage is a union of two people contributing positively through their love for each other. Together you must find answers for a variety of issues. **The breaking of a marriage is NOT like breaking a date.** The breaking of the marriage is painful and takes a heavy toll from your soul. Why is it different you might ask than breaking a date? Because when you are dating love doesn't truly develop until you are married and once married love grows deeper within. Love has an inner sanctuary all its own and when it dies from neglect, abuse, intolerance, or impatience, it painfully takes part of you until you recover.

Communication daily will keep this from ever happening. There are no perfect people in this world. Finding someone you want to be with, does not come along often in life. Treasure each other, help each other, and be patient with each other. The good times will outweigh the bad times. The transition into marriage takes time. Sometimes it takes a few years to fully understand who you married and what makes either of you happy or unhappy

~~~~~~~~~~~~~~~~~~~~~~~

Parallel Plane

What signs will be seen before either of you step onto a parallel plane? Be aware of the following "signs" when the *single plane* starts to develop into a *parallel plane*. Signs to be aware of how and when the parallel plane occurs:

- Sometimes it happens when you both rearrange your schedules using the time in the rearranged schedule differently than when it was exclusively set aside for the two of you and one of you miss that time of being together.

- Sometimes it happens when another priority (such as a promotion at work) replaces the attention and time that was given to the spouse.

- Sometimes it happens when the responsibilities of marriage overtake one's capability.

- Sometimes there just isn't any rest at home because of the obligations at home after a difficult day at work.

- Sometimes a mother or a father of a spouse or a family member becomes the priority permanently instead of the spouse.

- Sometimes friends of the wife or husband expect them to go out without the spouse often during the week.

- Sometimes joining an activity or a club demands the time that you had set aside for your spouse.

- Sometimes your spouse states they need to be alone? Why?

- Sometimes if the couple has animals such as: horses, dogs or exotic animals, the animals get more time and attention than the spouse.

- Sometimes your spouse has more interest in computer games than sleeping or being with their spouse.

When you were dating did you experience any sign of a parallel plane from your fiancée?

Fiancée - Explain: _____

_____

_____

_____

Fiancée - Explain: _____

_____

_____

_____

If you did see any parallel plane traits in your fiancée, do you think it will get better or worse once you are

married? Fiancée - Explain: _____

_____

_____

_____

Fiancée - Explain: _____

_____

_____

_____

Once you become aware you are on a parallel plane you can go back to when you were dating and you will

step off the parallel plane onto the single plane.   What you both enjoyed doing together will be the same,

and new activities of being together can be added, such as: Art Festivals, Museums, or Théâtre

Performances, enrolling in a Gym, Bowling, Playing Golf, Tennis or Bridge will make the time you both have

together very special.

The key is finding time to be together.

~~~~~~~~~~~~~~~~~~~~~~~

Procrastination

Questions for both of you to answer.

As a procrastinator, it is impossible to keep a promise because meaning to do something and not getting around to it impedes the promise. Procrastination is a major hindrance to promises.

What is procrastination? Explain: _____

_____

_____

_____

Why is procrastination a difficult behavior to live with? Explain: _____

_____

_____

_____

Many times, the procrastination of the individual is because they cannot remember what they said they will do, or will do it at another time, or they are not ready to do what they said they would do. This is very dangerous for a marriage because it is easy to lose respect for a procrastinator. Just the experience could turn you into fault finding of them, or even worse develop a dislike for the procrastinator. I have come up with a process that sometimes it works and other times it does not, but the 50% it works is a benefit for the procrastinator. Write a note of what must be done and lay it on the floor where they must step on it, when it is very important make half page notes and put it in every doorway they must step through!

~~~~~~~~~~~~~~~~~~~~~~~

Priorities – What's Important? - Third issue that trouble a marriage.

Priorities are very important and must be reviewed often as they change quickly and sometimes do not change back to what is the most important priority for either of you. May I suggest you **never take each other off the top of the priority list.** There will be times when the top priority might be shared for a given time with another priority, but neither of you should be off the top of the list permanently. Getting to know each other priorities will help with your own priorities. Always remember both of you will be each other's top priority.

Questions for both of you to answer

What are your top priorities? _____

_____

_____

_____

Getting to know each other will allow you to see what is important and a priority to your partner.

Are either of you organized or unorganized? Explain: _____

_____

_____

_____

In what areas are either of you organized or unorganized? Explain: _____

_____

_____

_____

Are either of you an early riser or late riser in the morning? Explain: _____

_____

_____

Are either of you early to bed or late to bed? Explain: _____

_____

_____

Are either of you a helpmate? Explain: _____

_____

_____

Do either of you want to go to worship over the week-end? Explain: _____

_____

_____

Do you both go to the same worship denomination? Explain: _____

_____

_____

Are either of you active in your church? Explain: _____

_____

_____

Are either of you active in the community? Explain: _____

_____

_____

What is your favorite pastime? Explain: _____

_____

_____

Do either of you like your eggs poached, scrambled, or fried? Explain: _____

_____

_____

Do either of you like to eat breakfast, lunch, or dinner early or late? Explain: _____

_____

_____

Do either of you like to read? Explain: _____

_____

_____

Do you share the same interests? Explain: _____

_____

_____

Do either of you want total control of all situations? Explain: _____

_____

_____

Did you know that if you want total control, you negate having a partner? Explain: _____

_____

_____

What foods do you or your partner dislike? _____

_____

_____

What foods are either of you allergic to? _____

_____

_____

What health issues do either of you have? _____

_____

_____

What health issues have either of you had in the past? _____

_____

_____

_____

_____

_____

_____

_____

_____

_____

_____

_____

_____

_____

_____

_____

_____

~~~~~~~~~~~~~~~~~~~~~~~

Criticism

One major factor in a marriage that need fixing right away is criticism. It comes in many forms. Verbally is very destructive to one's self-image and it can be over many issues from folding a sweater to drying the dishes. Very few individuals perform the same task identically.

The worst offense is when you ask for help and the help you receive is not up to your standards and you criticize them.

They may never try to help you again! *It is better to say thank you and change it later yourself!* Criticism can be avoided with good communication when a request is made. An explanation must be complete concerning the request; such as, when your partner requests all the spoons, forks, and knives be in separate compartments in the dishwasher. If this is not communicated the mixing of the utensils is not only an irritant to your partner but may keep the individual from ever loading or emptying the dishwasher again!

A marriage is like a home! Even in a new home within a few years, and sometimes in months, your home will need to be repaired. Good marriages are like a home and need repairing from time to time.

~~~~~~~~~~~~~~~~~~~~~~

How do you repair a marriage?

I use a simple formula! Both of you will have a blank piece of paper and a pen. Write down 3 things that are positive traits about your partner and 3 things that are negative traits about your partner. On the positive side begin with a little thing you like and then move on to more major behaviors. On the negative side begin with a little thing you dislike and then move onto more major traits. You then exchange the papers and read aloud each group to each other. The number one item on the negative side for each one listed on their paper must be worked on immediately. The other two listed traits on the negative side will eventually be listed separately as number one. This warning will give you time to start to find a way to correct your other negative traits.

When repairing a marriage, your partner does not want all your free time, or all your work time, or all your money, they only want YOU.

On days, you are mentally dull or emotionally flat...

> **Say a prayer which will keep you contented.**
>
> **Surrender to peace.**

Remember you are the co-pilot and God is the pilot, if you do not believe this statement plan and see how it works out!

Everyone can change small habits that are not major issues. I saw a saying long ago that stated, *"If nothing ever changed, there would be no butterflies"!*

~~~~~~~~~~~~~~~~~~~~~~~

Cold Feet

If either of you during the planning of a marriage does NOT want to get married...

"IF either of you decide you do not want to get married during the planning of your marriage." Not wanting to get married is different than the "jitters" of getting married. Nerves and jitters are the same. **Not wanting to get married means something is wrong, a red flag.** It is time for you to pause and explain what you are questioning. **Both of you should consider not getting married if it could it be one of the following?**

Your emotions stood in the way of your intellect when you made your decision.

Explain:_____

_____

_____

You are marrying for *dependency* because you need a *provider* or *something else*. Explain: _____

_____

_____

_____

You are marrying for idolization verses who they really are. *In other words, are you seeing them for who they really are or are you convincing yourself that they are more than who they really are?*

Explain: _____

_____

_____

Who Am I About to Marry?

Do you have a consciousness in the awareness of yourself?

Explain: _____

_____

Do you have a wish to escape from yourself *(an unwanted self)* and into the other?

Explain:_____

_____

Is there a need in you that you have mistakenly assumed is a reality for your fiancée? *In other words, do you have the need to be married and you mistakenly assume your fiancée does too*

Explain:_____

_____

Do you have a desire to search for gratification one desire after another? *(Addictions) Because love is always at home with itself and not looking elsewhere for other gratifications*

Explain:_____

_____

A self-aware person can love a non-aware person but the reverse is impossible. **Love comes with an awakening.** Explain: _____

_____

_____

The person you are about to marry seems different then the person you first met and fell in love with?

Explain: _____

_____

_____

Is there something else? Explain: _____

_____

There are many reasons that one would marry. Check off the ones that could apply to you.

Sexual attraction _____

Protection _____

Notoriety _____

Social position _____

Prestige _____

Gratitude _____

Pity _____

Spite _____

Adventure _____

Love _____

Economic security _____

Desire of home and family _____

Emotional Security _____

Parents _____

Escape from loneliness _____

Escape from parental home situation _____

Money _____

Companionship _____

Are any of your reasons that you checked marked above give you a reason to get married or give you a reason not get married? Explain: _____

_____

Common interests are not alone a sufficient basis on which to build a successful marriage. Sometimes they are confused with interest in the other person. Do you have different backgrounds that you are now realizing? **Check the ones that apply to you and use your journal to expand more.**

Cultural Background _____

Educational Pursuits _____

Vocational Choice _____

Different circles of friends _____

Do not want to be the last one to marry in your circle of friends _____

Do you think something is missing between the two of you? Explain: _____

_____

_____

_____

What are the three top qualities you are looking for in a partner?

1._____

2._____

3._____

When you decide you are attracted to an individual and they do **NOT** have **YOUR** top 3 things that make you happy, **STOP!** This is a **RED Flag!**

If your top three qualities are not met, none of the other traits a person has can possibly take their place. You will end up settling and no one is ever truly happy settling. Finding the right person is very important.

If your priority is not a relationship with God, it **SHOULD BE**, otherwise you are giving the individual Carte Blanche, which means full discretionary power over their behavior to satisfy their desires and wants with or without you.

~~~~~~~~~~~~~~~~~~~~~~~

The History of Marriage

Most individuals know their reason of wanting to be married, but many do not know the history of marriage. Marriage is a very ancient institution. In the Bible, Adam refers to Eve as his wife. This allows us to assume marriage is as old as humanity. Eve created from the rib of Adam equates to her life being created by human substance, and that underscores the common nature she shares with man and the bond that unites them. *Therefore, a man leaves his father and mother and joins himself to his wife and becomes one body. Genesis 2:24.*

Marriage becomes a way by which God's love is made manifest in human life. Marriage is the most durable Institution known making sure the continuance of our moral values. Becoming one flesh in marriage implies more than a sexual union. It implies that a new body, a new oneness has been created. It is a relationship in which the individuals at their wedding are offered possibilities. The wedding indicates their readiness to do so. During the ceremony, the *"I do"* is the couples mutual promise agreement. Equality is implied in this promise. It is common during the ceremony for each to take hold of the others right hand. This establishes through a symbolic form a physical contact. We cannot assume the vows said in marriage are magic. One should understand what the vows mean in the declaration of the wedding ceremony. The opening statement, *"Dearly beloved, we are gathered together here in the sight of God..."* gives an awareness of God's presence.

What does this mean to you?

Fiancée - Explain: _____

_____

_____

_____

Fiancée - Explain: _____

_____

_____

_____

The couple declares the statement of promise as follows:

- They accept one another as they are (in sickness and in health).

- They will both love and respect each other despite possible short comings (for better or worse).

- They will exert a continued effort to make the marriage succeed (keep the only unto thee; to have and to hold from this day forward).

- They anticipate problems (wilt thou love each other for richer or poorer).

- That the marriage is an exclusive relationship (forsaking all others).

- That they permanently dedicate themselves to each other (keep thee as long as you live).

Following the statement of promise there is an exchange of rings, a token and symbol of the pledge made in the marriage vows. It is common to end the marriage ceremony with, *"Those whom God hath joined together let not man put asunder...."* along with the phrase, *"Until death do us part. "*

Do you understand your vows? Is there any vow you are unsure of and if so, why?

Fiancée - Explain: _____

_____

_____

_____

Fiancée - Explain: _____

_____

_____

_____

Because the marriage commitment is binding, it is imperative to understand, hasty marriages tend to end in failure.

~~~~~~~~~~~~~~~~~~~~~

Love Is... True Happiness

Do not allow anyone or anything to come between you and your love. It is rare to find!

At the end of our lives we will remember the individuals who have loved us and the individuals whom we have loved.

"What is love?" I was asked by a man on his second marriage. I knew he never experienced love as it comes with joy and tears, happiness and sorrow, disappointment and elation, forgiveness, and gratefulness. I did not want to tell him what he did not have. I simply said there were three levels of love and that he could choose from one of three levels.

1. The first level was love of ourselves
2. The second level was love for another person but for one's self-interest.
3. The third level was to unconditionally love another person

Unconditional Love

Unconditionally is how God loves us. It is difficult to unconditionally love our partner with their weaknesses, and it is as difficult for our partner to love us with our weaknesses. In marriage when both partners try to change and succeed by sacrifice, patience, and communication, it strengthens the marriage.

~~~~~~~~~~~~~~~~~~~~~~~

Love is True North.

        Treasure it,

                Appreciate it,

                        It is very rare to find,

                                and above all,

                                      Communicate!

Love is deep within us, an amazing inner sanctuary of the soul.

By reworking, rethinking and reviewing this workbook from time to time, your marriage will be happier and stronger because of your self-discovery regarding, "Who Am I About to Marry?"

~~~~~~~~~~~~~~~~~~~~~~~~

Letter Poems

Many years ago, and still to this day, I started writing letter poems to God even though I knew He already knew what I was going to write. I always ended my letter poems with "*Good Night My Lord*".

A following letter poems have been selected on varied topics for conversation or inspiration.

Daylight Ending- Stowe, Vermont

Leaving Cape Cod, we drove on the outskirts of Boston, knowing we would return to Boston soon.
We were tempted to go to Chinatown when we saw a sign, but did not as it was already noon.

We were finally on our way, when along the highway there were large Evergreen trees.
They lined the highway like tin soldiers as far as we could see.

Driving through the higher altitude of the Green Mountains, the Mountain Caps were clipped by clouds passing on high,
Below on the mountain roads were highway signs to watch for Moose and Bear passing by!

As we approached Stowe, the rain was starting to come down.
We drove directly to the lodge, that was very close to town.

We checked in, and asked for directions to the church and the schedule for week-end Mass.
No matter where we are in Europe or USA, we ask for the schedule for mass so when attending we would not be the last.

By the time we checked in torrents of rain was dripping from the sky,
With jackets overhead, we climbed the stairs by two's, because of the deep snows in winter the lodges sit up high.

With daylight ending and after an organic pizza from Picassos Pizza, we went back to the lodge to unpacked for the week ahead.
We turned in by midnight, as we were tired and ready for bed.

We remembered what a good time we had in Colorado when we were at Vail and Beaver-Creek a few years ago.
We like to go to ski villages when there isn't any snow.

Thank You, Lord because each day is a treasure to behold.

Good Night My Lord

Sunlight Shadows

Sunlight shadows at sundown,
Shade the yard all around.

Trees before me bending down,
Pine limb reaching for the ground.

Hand Painted Chinese planter is what I see,
With a Bleeding-Heart blooming for me.

Beautiful white blossoms on aged Jade tree,
Rubber plant blooming for all to see.

See no bird nor hear no tweets.
Just too hot as shadows creep.

Off to an Outreach Meeting to extend a greeting,
To wonderful people whose hearts are bleeding.

When Mercy surrounds us, love calms us.
Arms wrapped around us, brings heaven upon us.

Thank you, God, for your love giving hope,
You are near to help us cope.

Good Night My Lord

Giacomo Puccini - La Rondine

Puccini was born in a city where a piece of my heart abides,
In Lucca, Italy, where dear friends reside.

Puccini was given at birth the musician family code,
His father was the choir master and organist at San Martino church, a sizeable load.

When we visited San Martino's church it looked like a large cathedral hall,
With crosses under glass and oil paintings on the wall.

The height of the church within, gave acoustical sounds to the noise of our steps,
And the white marble on the church façade had been beautifully kept.

Napoleons sister had a palace in Lucca to abide,
Lucca's history goes back to Caesar who came to the fortress for meetings by and by.

Puccini was a Romeo, addicted to love, heard within his opera notes,
Puccini was a game hunter, collector of cars and motor boats.

When I was younger Verdi and Wagner were too heavy for me,
Puccini's operas were to me, rose pedals, blown glass and starched organdy.

While Puccini admired the abilities of Verdi and Wagner in their grand stylistic notes,
Life episodes gave him inspiration for the operatic notes he wrote.

The opera score was magical and we will buy a CD to hear more,
of the bittersweet passion wrapped up in this emotional score.

Thank you, Jesus, for the experience of this wonderful, serendipitous day.
Good Night My Lord

Fountain of Life

Have you ever primed a pump to get water from the ground?
When you read the Word of God, the Word primes the pump for eternal life, I found.

The first encounters with God's word, was Creation and man,
God's Words started a fountain within Man, like a gusher on the land.

The bigger the fountain within you, the more love you have to share with your brothers,
You must welcome God into your heart before the water springs forth for you to give to others.

The Word of God is the fountain of life which we daily need,
The more you understand God's way, the more love you will have to do good deeds.

Jesus said to the woman at the well, "No one who drinks the water I give will ever be thirsty again."
"The Water I give is like a Flowing Fountain that Gives Eternal Life within." (John,4 vs13)

'For with you is the Fountain of Life, "(Ps36vs9) and is the answer to your daily prayers,
Drink a cup of water from the flowing Fountain at breakfast and throughout the day to lighten all your cares.

Good Night My Lord

Spot Lighting

Sun spotlighting neighbors pine,
Golden sunbeams bathing pines.

Bark of pine glowing red,
Not on fire, but color instead.

Limbs are glowing with sunset hues,
just before the sunsets due.

Signs of fall are in the leaves,
Twin birch first to turn a leaf.

Here you are my God with me,
Above, besides and inside me.

A day means so much more to me,
Because at sunset I sit with Thee.

Every night your nature sings,
So much smarter than we who think.

Thank You for this perfect day,
We try so hard to do it your way.

Good Night My Lord

Stormy Sky

Thunder bursting from stormy sky,
With high winds blowing rain inside.

Covered screen on porch you see,
Sprayed cold rain all over me.

Storm has left as clouds rolled by,
Leaving soaked land and grass outside.

Twilight is coming very soon,
Tonight, there will be no light from moon.

Distance Noisy sounds around,
from highways going out of town.

Airplane flying overhead as coast is clear,
No storm around, nothing to fear.

Heavy rains slowed the traffic down,
for Labor Day traffic all over town.

Good Night My Lord

Artwork

When we look for You My Lord, You are easy to find,
Without You we're lost and so very blind.

How fortunate we are to connect with Thee,
You are the light that helps us to see.

Praise to You for this clear sunny day.
Thank You for Your loving way,
Keeps me at peace day after day.

I feel so good just to know you are here,
It erases all my doubts and fear.

Blue skies and sunshine all around me,
More beautiful Artwork I'll never see.

Good Night My Lord

Evening Time

Evening comes so fast these nights,
Must stop and turn on table lights.

Today, my Lord how did we do?
So many have had no time for you.

Can my day, when dedicated to Thee,
Count as a prayer to you from me?

You my God, are so good to me,
Just Your presence is all I need.

Good Night My Lord

Lefkada, Greece- Poem 1

Oh, my Lord! What a splendid night,
The moon in Greece is a marvelous sight.

The shirred sharp mountains reach so high,
That clouds surround the peaks each night.

The Ionian Sea and Spectacular bays,
Make driving a pleasure on these beautiful days.

We gave a ride up a steep mountain road,
To an old woman carrying a heavy load.

She touched my heart when it was time to help her get out,
And when our eyes met, it was You I saw in her heart.

She was very old and not in good health,
And from her smiling bright eyes it was love that I felt.

She left behind in the car precious tomatoes three,
We insisted she take them and she did from me.

She pulled from her apron an apple for me,
Fruit she had picked from an old apple tree.

My Husband told me to take it and so I did,
This old Greek lady I just had to kiss.

(Continued)

Continued-Lefkada, Greece – Poem 1- Page 2

At the moment I kissed her, a blossom came into my heart,
And we waved to each other as we had to depart.

Our languages were different and communication nil,
But the love in our hearts spoke to each other and we were filled.

A feeling so rich came into my being,
And since our encounter, I just have to sing.

You greeted us, My Lord, on that steep mountain slope,
And the encounter with your love filled us with hope.

Who would expect You, in a poor shabby person so old?
It was You I embraced, I know it so.

Thank You for coming to share Your love so I'd see,
Your kindness and love from that old woman to me.

Good Night My Lord

Lefkada, Greece – Poem #2

Lefkada has 25,000 people, with many shops and pleasant faces,
During the summer, it is a fast-paced busy place.

The Corinthians took control of the island in 640B.C. from Achaemenians until the British left in 1864,
It offers a variety from mountain villages to beach resorts with a main street filled with cafes and stores.

We treasured seeing Cleopatra's creek and Alexander the Great's water battle ground,
Along with coves and sandy beaches where summer resorts abound.

Vasiliki and Nidri are resorts we drove miles to reach,
And are a wind surfer's paradise at these resorts on the beach.

Lefkada is a perfect place to sail a ship,
With currents that can be managed so you never tip.

A sailor's delight among the bays and waterways,
Nowhere have we seen better sailing waters than around Polaros and Lefkada bays.

We ate where yachts dock when our lunch was due,
Scorpios island was near and within our view.

The historical markers show Lefkada's importance to the past,
In B.C. the port was very active and through repeated earthquakes the city lasts.

Thank You Lord, for allowing us to see B.C. of yesteryear,
I never dreamed I'd be so close to antiquity and stand so near.
Good Night My Lord

Spartacus

In the middle of surviving this busy season,
My husband surprised me with ballet tickets to "Spartacus", at the Fox Theatre this evening.

What a treat to see the Grigorovich ballet from Russia tonight,
The Art Direction, the Libretto and Choreography by Yuri Grigorovich was simply a delight.

Plutarch, the historian of the ancient world wrote of Spartacus in his book titled, "Lives",
It states, "Spartacus had honor, courage and strength, while Crassus voided his virtue with lust and gain, which he daily strived.

The unusual set and costume designs by Simon Vernalize born in 1909,
and the great music by Aram Khachaturian born in 1903, were classical finds.

The ballet had two acts with nine scenes that we did see,
Adapted from the novel by Raffaele Giovanni, which took place in ancient Rome in 1 B.C.

The conflicting figures of Spartacus and Crassus showed the clash of two different worlds
on earth waking fears,
And ends with the power of the Roman Legions crucifying Spartacus on their spear and leaving Phrygia in tears.

Spartacus became Yuri's signature work in 1968, a marvelous feat,
He worked as the Artistic Director for thirty years at the Bolshoi Ballet, giving Russia a treat.

Thank you, Jesus, for the difficult fast toe dancing of the ballet dancers we did see,
It was a difficult dance to master on their toes and feet.

Good Night My Lord

Sunset Spotlight

Sunlight lends its beams to trees,
While on the hilltop bathing leaves.

Like a flash bulb when bulb goes out,
Sunset spotlight moves about.

Sunlight rests on clouds above,
A glorious reflection of your love.

Lawn chairs and tables sitting out,
Oh! So nice when stars are out.

All good things belong to Thee,
Thank You for all you've shared with me.

Good Night My Lord

.

Die Walkure (1856)-The Ring of Nibelungs-The Valkyrie

A welcome surprise this evening, my husband treated me to,

A 110-piece Atlanta Symphony orchestra in tune.

Act III, "The Valkyrie" is a challenging score,

By Richard Wagner, a genius-self-obsessed and intolerant bore.

Act III," the Valkyrie" is the second opera of four,

"The Ring of Nibelungs," consists of four opera's lasting twelve hours or more.

In the opera Act III," The Valkyrie ", takes place before the emergence of human civilization's birth,

There are more than 100 symbolic themes that bind together this genius's work.

Writing the four Librettos' for the opera, were written backwards from the 4th to the 1st opera,

before the symphony he would create.

"The Ring" took 26 years to finish, as Wagner took a 12-year leave and "The Ring" had to wait.

The first two operas had already received their premiers in King Ludwig's Theater, on separate days.

The completed cycle of "The Ring", was postponed until Wagner's acoustical and physical facilities were

finished, so Wagner could have his way.

Wagner's Pan Tone use of ever changing harmony was the basis of atonal music of the day.

Other trends were developed in modern music, overshadowing Wagner's dominance in pan toned

Music, his exclusive way.

Thank You Lord for the exquisite multicolored ballgowns that the ten Soprano's wore,

And for the conductor of the San Francisco Opera, Donald Runnicles, who conducted a perfect score.

Good Night My Lord

Jerusalem

We have been in the city for one full week,
Walking the streets among Holy Places that we seek.

We saw King David's Tomb, the Upper Room and many Jerusalem Gates,
And MT. Olives and Caiaphas home where you endured your fate.

We had wished to walk your steps alone,
But that is impossible as thousands of feet are on your stones.

Rushing here and rushing there, put my prayer in the Wailing wall,
I reached so high to put my prayer between two bricks standing tall.

In the Arab section, we saw bedazzling candy on shelves, in a tiny space.
We sampled and bought candy with its heavenly taste.

Mosques, and Temples surround the Holy Sepulcher Church,
Giving the traveler a choice in their worship search.

We visited Chihuly's glass blown moon displayed over the Citadel wall,
It was the largest exhibition mounted in the Tower of David, 10,000 glass pieces in all.

Many differences within the old city divide,
but Art for a moment has united everyone on one side.

From our balcony, we can see the Holy city wall, lighted every night,
The Jerusalem wall is just beautiful with the Tower of David shedding light.

Thank you, Lord for this wonderful stay,
 it is difficult to close our eyes and sleep, even knowing tomorrow is another day.

Good Night My Lord

Golden Hue

Sunset Fading, golden hue,
Illuminates foliage, especially the new.

Humming bird strolling on pink brick,
I sit watching, It's such a kick.

Birds are flying over pine,
Last flight at sunset, before they dine.

Airplanes hidden with sound reaching down,
So high in the heavens, over the town.

Traffic is bustling, errands not done,
When day is over, it's time for fun.

No scorching heat but Cirrus star rising,
Predictions are for temperature rising.

No movement around me, quiet today,
Everything resting, it must be God's way.

Maybe I'm early, before twilight's hue,
That's when the prayers of song birds are due.

Thank You, dear Lord, for all you have given me,
It's time for my prayer to give thanks to three.

Good Night My Lord

Bless Us Tonight

Take care of the world Lord, as you usually do,
Fill all our hearts with the wonder of you.

The Power on earth is an empty reward,
When will we will take up your chaplet and put down our swords?

Why did you choose me to know you so well?
What do you want of me, when will you tell?

I'll write to you as long as I live,
I know you grace me with your power to give.

Your wonderful mystery is in the air,
I breathe you in daily, you are everywhere.

Bless us tonight with your Holy Grace,
Turn sinners to angels by your loving embrace.

Good Night My Lord

Grey Sky

Cold grey sky above evergreen tree,
Looks like a snow sky above me.

Cold grey sky blankets the day,
Snow sky shows it will be cold day.

A good meal is needed for all who are on the streets,
Hot soup tonight would be a real treat.

The abundance of our love is for those who need a lift,
It flows like a fountain when we share God's gifts.

MY prayers keep me grounded in my trust in you.
It is so easy to disconnect when life stresses are due.

Thank You for my life today,
I'm called each evening to simply pray.

Good Night My Lord

Peter and the Fish

The Bible is filled with great stories of wonder.
The following story is a good one to Ponder.

Often, we are tired when we are called to extend,
To help a neighbor, run an errand or listen to a friend.

Peter and his companions were exhausted from fishing without a catch all night.
After docking," they went to wash their nets" by the early morning light.
(Luke, Chapter 5vs 2)

Jesus, gave Peter a command to obey:
"To row out to the deep water and let your nets down to catch some fish" today. (Luke, chapter5vs4)

Peter was tired, but did not refuse Jesus's command that day,
He went beyond his own reasoning to overcome his exhaustion to obey.

Peter caught so many fish, his nets began to tear.
This would become the symbol of the Apostles future message that
Peter would be a fisher of men put in his care.

Remember when your struggle appears to great, impossible to achieve and
your faith is growing dim,
Turn toward God and have faith and trust in Him.

Good Night My Lord

Corfu, Greek Cafe

On the strip near the bay we found a café,
In torrents of rain we stopped one day.

We were early guests this rainy eve,
And on the menu, there were homemade dishes, we did read.

The hostess and cook motioned for us to the kitchen, to take a look,
Into the kitchen we went to see what they cooked.

There were drawers of fish and kettles of soup,
And the cook was real pretty with high energy too.

My husband pointed to our selection so there would be no doubt,
As our hostess spoke very little English to help us out.

Spiro, the owner came in through the door around eight.
He was a humble man and he sat with us as we ate.

Spiro and the cook were husband and wife,
They work together in a busy life.

Spiro could not speak English and we could not speak Greek but
somehow, we knew each other,
By the end of the week, he was our brother.

The mural on the wall depicted Spiros' Dad in a boat.
What a wonderful legacy that the restaurant is still afloat.
(continued)

Continued- Corfu, Greek café

The Restaurant was founded in 1920 by Spiros 'Dad on the Bay,
Ninety years later, in the same location has stayed.

What wonderful fun we had eating time after time,
With homemade desert sent by his Mom when we dined.

Spiro introduced us to his friend "Spiro", while we dined,
A generous man who shared with us candy and wine.

Both Spiro's taught us how to eat fish eyes.
When it was suggested, I asked him why?

It was a family affair when we arrived to eat,
belonging to a Greek family is a wonderful treat.

Thank You Dear Lord, for all of our fun.
We had a good time with the Fisherman's son.

Good Night My Lord

Bethlehem

Long ago, in Wisconsin, with icicles on window panes,

Christmas trees were decorated with lights and candy canes.

Our town decorated streetlights with huge pine bough wreaths,

And sometimes there was five feet of snow upon our streets.

Christmas was a festive time when Bethlehem became part of our celebration time,

There were Mangers in our homes, and larger Mangers in our churches heralding your sign.

In a hundred years I never would have thought I would visit Bethlehem someday too.

When we did, we traveled through the desert, like the three kings who came to worship you.

It was a long way to Bethlehem by Taxi from Jerusalem, where we were bound,

And entering Bethlehem a large city, there was construction all around.

We parked above the Shepherd's field and walked up many steps quite steep,

to the Cathedral of the Nativity, A huge Cathedral which was empty of all seats!

We entered by the side door, as the stable was inside a large cathedral wall.

The lines at the Cathedral front door wrapped around the block, but our taxi driver knew where to enter

without waiting, in the back, to see your stall.

When we entered, we stepped into the stable, it was small and a crowded place.

I kissed the STAR upon the floor where you were born in this teeny-tiny space.

You changed the earth that blessed day,

When you came to show us a new way.

Continued.

(continued-Bethlehem Page 2

Leaving Bethlehem for Jerusalem was very stressful for me,

Checkpoints and guns on Arab land made me as nervous as I could be.

The boundary of Jordan had miles of barbed- wire along the turf,

And was mined with explosives laid in the earth.

 I cannot tell an Arab or a Jew apart,

They look alike because they both came from Abraham's seed and heart.

Good Night My Lord

One Foundation

You might ask how it can be that Jesus dwells in you and me?
It is by the scriptures that we read, and by our actions and our deeds.

Jesus is known to his flock.
One foundation has been built on the Sacred Rock.

There is one foundation we build upon with-in,
It is rooted and fused with love to share with all women and men.

There are many churches all around,
And God has not been divided, I have found.

Those who have God within, are living stones who are building a foundation of great worth.
Let us ask our Neighbors and Kin to become living stones to help build God's Kingdom on earth.

Good Night My Lord

~~~~~~~~~~~~~~~~~~~~~~~

Letters

*The following stories have been written by individuals who offered to write how the **Separated and Divorce Support Group** and **Workbooks** helped them gain new perspectives on relationships for their future.*

Who Am I About to Marry: by Charlotte

I have *"Been there, Done that!"* when it comes to marriage. Unfortunately, my first go- around was an unsuccessful attempt. In the beginning, my ex-husband and I seemed to have a lot in common as far as our backgrounds and how we were raised. We looked good on paper, but in real life we were not a match. That became evident shortly after we exchanged our vows. We got engaged much too quickly without getting to really know each other. It turns out we were very ill-suited for one another and probably remained together, unhappily, far too long (over a dozen years). I had always believed marriage was a one-time deal, no turning back. But it was a miserable situation that became intolerable, especially after children entered the equation.

Thankfully, the Separated and Divorce support group at my church and the facilitator's first workbook, **"Conquering Divorce with God"** helped pull me through. With the Author's help and the group's support, I not only survived, but thrived. I find myself in a much better place.

Now here I am four and one-half years later considering marriage again. My heart is definitely open to the possibility. Through time, experience, life's lessons and the author's latest workbook, **"Who Am I About to Marry?"** I have more confidence and trust in myself that I'll get married right the second time. Her workbook helped me learn more about myself, my core values, principles and boundaries. I've also learned some important questions to consider and ask my significant other.

Continued

Continued-by Charlotte

It is necessary to take the rose-colored glasses off when we're considering such an important decision as marriage. The facilitator's workbook takes a very realistic approach-delving into some very real and oftentimes uncomfortable topics of discussion like finances and parenting styles. It also pinpoints some early signs of trouble to look for and avoid-like living on parallel planes. I wish I had this valuable resource before I dove into my first marriage. I can definitely see the red flags now.

I'm not looking for perfect. I'm looking for the one I can accept and who accepts me for all our strengths, quirks and even flaws. I've been exclusively dating a man the last few years who has grown very important to me. We've both have gotten past painful divorces and have six children between us. I prefer my life with him in it. He's good for me and my children. We've discussed marriage. It's something we're working toward. I'm very optimistic. This workbook has helped give me a sense of confirmation and peace.

Thank you, Pattie!

Charlotte

I Was Happily Married for 23 Years and Want That Again: By Lea

I was happily married for 23 years and want that again! Somehow, I missed the warning signs along the way and I wanted to equip myself with the knowledge and become wiser on choosing my next mate. Along with this workbook, *"Who Am I About to Marry?"* and Pattie's previous workbook, *"Conquering Divorce with God,"* helped me get my confidence back and feel more in control of my future. The workbook, *"Who Am I About to Marry?"* brought up topics for my mate & I to discuss that are critical to know about each other concerning view points on life & handling situations we will have to face. The questions forced us to discuss issues now as opposed to later. Instead of glossing over a topic we had to thoroughly discuss it, which was beneficial to get to really know each other better. I believe the major component *"Who Am I About to Marry"* workbook helped my mate and I do was, **communicate**.

There were certainly topics we didn't agree on, for example, finances. I had one view point and he had another, which created tension between us, but with the questions this chapter asked, it helped us through our issues step by step. Another important section was *Careers- Equal treatment and Respect* because it talked about jobs in the workplace as well as at home. Once again, the questions walked us through our issue's step by step and got us talking about different issues. An issue came up about a possible job change in the future, which I would have not been aware of, if not for the question. The topics, some easy to talk about & some are not, the questions are sometimes uncomfortable to answer & make you think, but are important to get you both to communicate.

Another important section was the *Personal Inventory* section, because you list what is important to you and your mate. I did this section in the previous workbook *"Conquering Divorce with God".* *A workbook that I would highly recommend for those healing after divorce.*   It was beneficial in rebuilding my life and giving me a direction in repairing the sadness divorce left in my life. The questions in that workbook, helped me put the pieces in my life back in order. That workbook talks about divorce being like a bridge you have to walk over it and go through the emotions in order to get to the other side.

continued

<u>**Continued by Lea**</u>

<u>**It is important to heal from a divorce or a long-term relationship before you can let someone else in your life.**</u> This workbook was the first step in getting my life to where it is now. I would suggest this workbook for anyone who needs to heal from the emotions and scars a divorce can leave behind.

After going through the workbook "***Who Am I About to Marry?***" I feel better equipped & secure in knowing that there is a future with my mate and can be reassured that I am making the right decision. One of the greatest lines in the workbook is in the ***Differences Between Us*** section, *"It is important when you become aware of differences between you and your partner that you communicate with your partner as soon as these differences arise".*

Communication is the key to a successful marriage. Everyone is going to have differences but if communicated it will not be a major issue. I highly recommend this book and consider it a must for anyone thinking about getting engaged or married.

–Lea

HI, My Name is Robert,

It was after 23 years of marriage that I found myself divorced. What a hand life had dealt me. What should I do? Where will I go? How will I get through this? I never thought I would find myself here. We vowed *"until death do us part".* When I realized I couldn't get through this on my own, I began to seek help. A friend referred me to Saint Joseph Catholic Church where there was a divorce group that met every Wednesday evening to see if the Support Group and facilitator could help me. Little did I know how those meetings would change my life forever. I met with Pattie the facilitator, one Wednesday evening to see if she could help me. I wasn't sure if this was the forum for me. But later, as the weeks went by, I began to feel more comfortable each time it was my turn to speak. Being a support group of men and women in the same situation gave me a feeling that I was not alone and soon the healing began. Pattie with her support, patience and dedication to each member of the group, both individually and collectively lifted us to a level of confidence and self-esteem that we had not had in quite some time. She gave us confidence that there is life after divorce.

Many months later I was able to return to a social life and began to date again. It took a long time but I remembered what Pattie would say to us about the "Big 3" found in her workbook, *"Conquering Divorce with God"*. I put my trust in God to send me someone who would be my life partner. It didn't happen overnight. In fact, it took several years. But in His time, I met a woman who I would fall in love with. We married. I kept to my values. I have returned to my relationship with God realizing all things are possible trough Him. Life is good!

The **Separated and Divorced Ministry** and the building blocks in her workbooks, that Pattie uses to help people get through this difficult time has truly been a God send to me and many others who have been in her care. God Bless this dear lady. I will always be grateful to her.

Robert

~~~~~~~~~~~~~~~~~~~~~~~~

About the Author

Pattie Atkinson Scotto

- Award Winning Business Leader
- Speaker
- Leader for over 25 years for the support group *Partners Left Behind in Separation or Divorce*
- Author and Poet, Pattie authored the *"Conquering Divorce with God"* Workbook and *"Who Am I About to Marry?"* Workbook *(both available on Amazon)*
- Principal with Key Recruiters, keyrecruitersusa.com

If you are interested in a speaker, class, or help in starting a support group, email
Keyjobs@bellsouth.net
Facilitators Guide Available

**Workbooks are available on Amazon or email
keyjobs@bellsouth.net**

Group discount at keyjobs@bellsouth.net

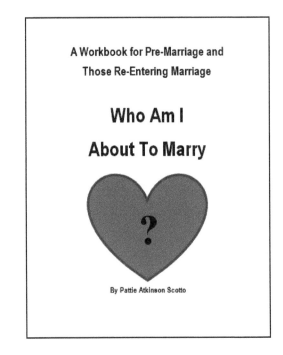

A Workbook for Pre-Marriage and Those Re-Entering Marriage

Who Am I About To Marry

By Pattie Atkinson Scotto